Josef Schroer

A Feast of Temptation

Chocolate

Cookery Editor Sonia Allison

Series Editor Wendy Hobson

foulsham

Foreword

It was Quetzacoatl, the feathered serpent god of air and water, who passed on what were considered magic seeds – actually cacao beans – personally to the Aztecs. So well before Columbus reached Central America, the people were drinking a kind of unsweetened 'soup' made from those seemingly heaven-sent and highly-prized beans known as xoccoat.

Through the Spanish conquistadores, cacao beans reached the Spanish court and then began their triumphal journey into other parts of Europe. Inventive and creative minds quickly learned how to refine raw xoccoat and cleverly adapted it to suit European tastes, which were taking on a growing sophistication. In 1836, France alone converted 3,000 tonnes of raw chocolate into drinks and confectionery, and in 1880, the Swiss started manufacturing their own unmistakeable type of rich chocolate, perhaps a little softer than it is now, but always high quality and much sought-after. The rest is history.

Contents

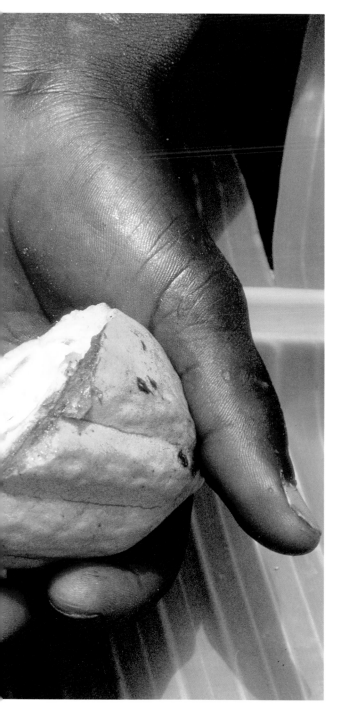

All About Chocolate

It is perhaps surprising that though most people love chocolate, very few would recognise it in its raw state, so here is a little about how it comes to us and how we can use it in our cooking.

From the Bean to the Chocolate

It is some sort of miracle that an international luxury such as chocolate can be made from the cacao bean, as in its natural state it is both bitter and inedible.

The tropical cacao trees grow well where there is both heat and humidity and thrive happily in South America and parts of Africa, as well as other places with a similar climate. The fruit is long and oval and has a hard and rough skin, with the colour varying from green-yellow to red-brown. The inside of each is filled with white flesh in which about 20 to 40 beans are embedded. Throughout one year around 3 kg of beans can be harvested from one tree.

Well known types of cocoa are Criollo and Forastero but the Criollo tree is the better of the two and its beans are used for the very finest chocolate. The tree is, however, highly sensitive to changes in the weather and the harvest is affected accordingly.

After the harvest the fruit is taken away for fermentation. After a swift blow from a machete, the fruit is opened and the beans are scraped out of the flesh. The fermentation process that follows is decisive in extracting high quality raw cocoa, and, depending on the type of bean, this fermentation lasts from two to six days. This process prevents the seeds from germinating, while it also removes the bitter substances and the typical cocoa flavour is allowed to develop. The fermented raw cocoa is washed, dried and sorted for quality. Packed in jute sacks, the cocoa makes its long journey by sea to the ports of Europe and North America.

When the beans arrive at their destination they are cleaned and roasted, making the cocoa itself easier to digest. Above all, however, the taste and flavour is refined and improved. An important part of roasting is also the removal of the husk and the germ from the beans. The heat loosens the husk which becomes brittle and flakes off, a process now carried out in huge machines. Using blasts of air and suction units of different strengths, the beans, husks and shoots are separated from each other. The beans are ground finely in special mills which produce a thick paste that solidifies on cooling. While the cocoa is being ground, different types of bean are blended according to the quality demanded in the finished product. The cocoa mixture is then ready for further processing.

The ground cocoa paste can now be made into chocolate, cocoa powder and cocoa butter. By pressing the cocoa mixture, cocoa butter is

produced, cocoa powder is left. The basic ingredients for confectionery are now ready: the cocoa mixture for making chocolate, cocoa butter for hard cooking chocolate, and cocoa powder for use in drinks and baking.

In order to make chocolate, the cocoa mixture is processed with cocoa butter, sugar and, depending on the recipe, with different flavourings (such as vanilla) in large mixing machines. The sugar content in plain chocolate is about 40 per cent and in milk chocolate 50 per cent. The mixture is subsequently put through large rollers by which it is squeezed into very small pieces. The chocolate is finally transferred to large tubs where it is moved backwards and forwards for two to three days. In this way it develops its typical characteristics which are its soft melt and clean breaking quality. The chocolate is heated to a temperature of 50 to 80°C and the addition of lecithin makes it more malleable.

Notes on the Recipes

1 Follow one set of measurements only, do not mix metric and Imperial.
2 Eggs are size 2.
3 Spoon measurements are level.
4 Kcals refer to one portion of the recipe and are approximate.
5 Preparation times include both preparation and cooking and are approximate.

Types of Chocolate

Household Cooking Chocolate
This is good value for money. The chocolate ingredients have been carefully blended and rolled but the quality is not particularly high. This is often reflected in the price.

Plain Chocolate
This dark chocolate is pleasant both in cooking and to eat. It is easy to melt for the home cook.

Milk Chocolate
This is chocolate to which milk powder has been added. Other additions can include nuts, raisins and candied fruits.

Filled Chocolate
Sometimes chocolate is made with a variety of fillings. Fruit paste or whole fruit, liqueur or other flavourings are enclosed inside the processed chocolate. The separation between filling and chocolate is usually clear, especially, for example, where a white peppermint cream or violet cream is encased in darker chocolate.

White Chocolate
This is made from cocoa butter, milk, sugar and flavourings. It contains no cocoa mixture and therefore remains white.

Couverture Chocolate
This is basically a confectioner's chocolate, used in the production of high quality goods, and contains a higher proportion of cocoa butter than is generally found in other chocolate. It is not intended for eating but is used by the manufacturing industry for sweets, chocolates, cakes, biscuits, fancy gâteaux and ice cream. It is sold in blocks which experts process before using.

Essential Equipment

In order to work professionally with chocolate you will need some special equipment. This is listed below.

Water Bath or Bain Marie
In order to melt chocolate easily, you need a water bath. You can buy one the professionals use from a speciality kitchen shop or simply make your own by standing a bowl or basin over a pan of gently simmering water and leaving the chocolate in the bowl until it melts.

Kitchen Scales
Kitchen scales are useful, especially the electronic ones which are capable of weighing small amounts accurately.

Food and Sugar Thermometer
This is an important piece of equipment as chocolate should not be heated above 44°C, otherwise it loses its gloss.

Food Processor
A food processor with different settings will make working with chocolate considerably easier.

Palette Knife and Spatula
One of these will be required to smooth out chocolate icing, or to make chocolate flakes or curls.

Dipping Fork
Available in different sizes from catering suppliers, these hold small portions of food for you while you dip them into melted chocolate.

Chocolate Moulds
Chocolate moulds can be used to produce decorative chocolate shapes or hollows which can later be filled.

Marble Work Surface
Because of its coolness and smooth surface, a marble slab is ideal for working with chocolate.

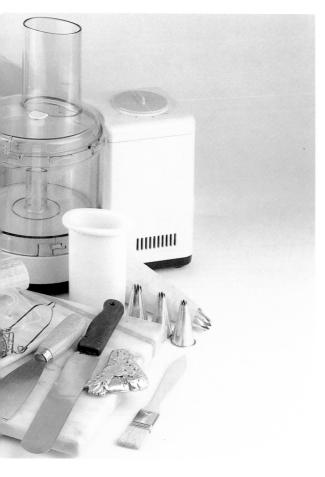

Working with Chocolate

Firstly, a few words on storage. Chocolate likes to be kept dry and cool and if subjected to warmth and damp for too long, will develop a fat or sugar lime coating which the professionals describe as greyness: a dull bloom on the outside. This is not harmful; it is NOT mould but it does spoil the appearance of the chocolate. Another point worth noting, is that chocolate readily absorbs aromas so it should be kept well away from strong-smelling foods.

Tempering Couverture Chocolate

In this process the couverture develops a high gloss and anything covered with it will not then have a milky or grey appearance.

1 Break the chocolate into pieces and place in a bowl. Melt in a water bath or in a bowl or basin over hot water.

2 Pour two-thirds of the melted couverture on to the marble work surface. Leave the remainder aside temporarily.

3 Using a spatula, knead the melted chocolate on the marble work surface until the mixture begins to thicken.

4 Still using the spatula, return the chocolate mixture to the rest of the melted couverture and stir thoroughly with a wooden spoon. Only at this stage should the couverture be used for coating or glazing. Milk chocolate should reach a temperature of 28°C and plain chocolate 30°C.

Coating

When coating large items, it is important to work quickly and effectively as otherwise the chocolate becomes 'blind', that is, it loses its gloss.

1 Place the cake or gâteau on a wire mesh rack. The cake should be cold and have a firm surface.

2 Temper the couverture and always make a little more than you think you will need as there is nothing worse than having insufficient available for your immediate needs. Pour the melted couverture over the whole cake, making sure there are no uncovered areas. Smooth evenly with a palette knife.

Dipping

As this process takes a little longer, it is important to keep the couverture constantly at the correct temperature. The best thing to do is to use either a water bath or a bowl or basin over hot water. Kept warm like this, the couverture will stay liquid.

1 Larger items that only need part-covering with couverture can be dipped by hand. They can then be placed on a wire mesh rack to harden.

2 When you want to cover small items completely, hold them securely with a dipping fork then twirl round gently in the melted couverture.

Chocolate Curls and Chips (Raspings)

These are quite easy and fun to make after a little practice.

1 Temper the couverture in a water bath or in a basin over hot water and spread it out thinly on a marble slab with a palette knife.

2 As soon as it begins to harden, scrape up the chocolate with a palette knife. Depending on the hardness and thickness of the chocolate, short or long chips and curls can be produced.

Cut-Out Chocolate Figures

In order to cut out chocolate figures there are two methods you can use.

1 Place the tempered chocolate on greaseproof paper, spread smoothly with a palette knife and wait until it starts to harden.

2 Cut into shapes with cutters, kept warm in a very cool oven. The cutters MUST NOT BE ALLOWED to get hot or the chocolate will melt.

Moulded and Hollow Chocolate Shapes

A number of different moulds can be bought from speciality shops. Moulds are used primarily to make filled chocolates but are not that easy for the non-professional cook to use.

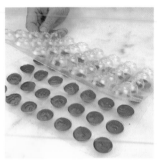

1 Ensure the moulds are polished clean before the chocolate is poured in. If not, you will be unable to remove the chocolate hollows from their moulds.

2 Close the moulds and let the chocolate cool. After removing, the hollow chocolates can be filled with creams, truffle mixtures and so on.

Chocolate Leaves

These make unusual garnishes for desserts.

1 Take a number of green leaves, wash them carefully and dry on kitchen paper. Dip the upper side of each leaf into melted, tempered chocolate or into good quality, melted plain chocolate.

2 Place the undersides of the leaves on a plate or a piece of foil and leave the chocolate to harden. Afterwards, carefully pull away the leaves from the set chocolate. The veins of the leaves will now be clearly visible.

Piping Accessories

You can either pipe patterns directly on to a cake or gâteau or pipe them separately on to non-stick parchment paper. The decorations may then be transferred when cold and set but need careful handling as they fracture easily.

3 Turn over the remaining points and the piping bag can be filled with a liquid, tempered chocolate or with any other suitable piping mixture.

5 Draw a few designs on to a piece of paper. Lay a sheet of greaseproof paper on top and outline with piped chocolate. Leave to harden and set before removing.

1 In order to produce clean piping, a piping bag is essential. It is easy enough to make your own. Fold a square of greaseproof paper into a triangle and cut it at the fold with a sharp knife.

4 Fold the top part of the piping bag over so that it encloses the filling. Cut away a fraction of the paper from the pointed end to make a hole. This may be large, medium or small, depending on the type of decoration you want. Roll up the folded part of the bag (the top) and use as demonstrated.

6 Use a thin knife or palette knife to loosen the decorations carefully away from the paper. Transfer to cakes, gâteaux or desserts.

2 Roll up the paper from one side to the other, keeping your thumb in the top opening.

Biscuits and Cakes

Nothing is more special to serve to your guests than home-made chocolate biscuits or cakes. Here is a special selection for you to try – from the simple to the more adventurous.

Chocolate Twists

Makes 36
Preparation time: 1¹/₂-2 hours
150 kcal/630 kJ

For the dough:

500 g/1 lb 2 oz/4¹/₄ cups plain flour

300 g/11 oz/1¹/₃ cups butter, softened

200 g/7 oz/1³/₄ cups caster sugar

5 ml/1 tsp grated lemon rind

10 ml/2 tsp ground cinnamon

a few drops of rum flavouring

10 ml/2 tsp vanilla essence

2 eggs, beaten

For covering:

100 g/4 oz plain chocolate, melted

100 g/4 oz milk chocolate, melted

---

1 Sift the flour into a bowl. Rub in the butter then stir in the sugar. Add the lemon rind, cinnamon, rum and vanilla essence. Gradually work in the eggs. Using cold hands, lightly knead the ingredients together to form a pliable dough.
2 Place in a bowl, cover with a damp cloth and leave to rest in the refrigerator for about 1 hour.
3 Remove the dough and divide into three equal pieces. Roll out into long cords and cut each cord into 12. Twist the ends of each piece together and press into a pretzel shape.
4 Arrange the biscuits on a greased baking tray and bake in a preheated oven at 200°C/400°F/gas mark 6 for 10 to 15 minutes. Leave to cool on a wire rack.
5 Cover the biscuits with the melted chocolate. Transfer to a sheet of greaseproof paper and leave to harden in a cool place.

Photograph opposite (bottom)

Chocolate Rings

Makes 36
Preparation time: 40-50 mins
280 kcal/1175 kJ

For the dough:

400 g/14 oz/1³/₄ cups butter, softened

350 g/12 oz marzipan

3 egg whites

30 ml/2 tbsp Maraschino liqueur

25 g/1 oz/2 tbsp caster sugar

400 g/14 oz/3¹/₂ cups plain flour

50 g/2 oz/¹/₂ cup cocoa powder

For decoration:

200 g/7 oz white chocolate, melted

45 ml/3 tbsp butter or margarine

200 g/7 oz/1³/₄ cups almonds, chopped

---

1 Beat the butter with the marzipan until creamy. Whisk the egg whites with the Maraschino liqueur until very stiff then gradually fold in the sugar, a little at a time. Fold the egg whites carefully into the marzipan mixture using a wooden spoon. Mix the flour and the cocoa powder together, sieve and fold carefully into the marzipan mixture.
2 Fill a piping bag with the mixture and pipe out rings of 5 cm/2 ins diameter on to a greased baking sheet. Bake in a preheated oven at 200°C/400°F/gas mark 6 for 10 to 15 minutes. Remove to a rack and leave to cool.
3 Coat tops of the biscuit rings with melted chocolate and transfer to a wire rack.
4 Heat the butter in a frying pan, add the almonds and fry briefly until golden. Sprinkle over the rings and leave in a cool place to dry completely.

Photograph opposite (top)

Cocoa Tongues

Makes 12
Preparation time: 50 mins
525 kcal/2205 kJ

For the dough:

*225 g/**8 oz**/1 cup butter,
softened*

*100 g/**4 oz**/¹/₂ cup caster
sugar*

3 eggs

*25 g/**1 oz**/¹/₄ cup cornflour*

*25 g/**1 oz**/¹/₄ cup cocoa*

*5 ml/**1 tsp** ground cinnamon*

*250 g/**9 oz**/2¹/₄ cups plain
flour, sifted*

For the filling and covering:

*200 ml/**7 fl oz**/scant 1 cup
whipping cream*

*150 g/**5 oz** milk chocolate,
melted*

*5 ml/**1 tsp** rum*

*200 g/**8 oz** plain chocolate,
melted*

1 Beat the butter to a soft
cream with the sugar then
gradually add the un-
beaten eggs. Beat until
the mixture is light and
fluffy. Fold in the remaining dough ingredients.
2 Pipe 9 cm/3¹/₂-in
lengths of dough on to a
greased baking sheet.
Bake in a preheated oven
at 200°C/400°F/gas mark
6 for 10 to 15 minutes.
3 Melt the cream and
chocolate. Add the rum,
leave to cool then beat
until creamy.
4 Sandwich together the
tongues in pairs, with the
filling then coat with
melted chocolate.

Photograph (left)

Chocolate Crunch

Makes 12
Preparation time: 45 mins
340 kcal/1430 kJ

For the dough:

3 egg whites

250 g/*9 oz*/1 ½ cups icing sugar, sifted

150 g/*5 oz*/1 ¼ cups almonds, chopped

40 g/1 ½ *oz*/3 tbsp butter

30 ml/*2 tbsp* cocoa powder

2.5 ml/*½ tsp* cinnamon

5 ml/*1 tsp* vanilla essence

30 ml/*2 tbsp* brandy

5 ml/*1 tsp* grated lemon rind

50 g/*2 oz* candied lemon rind, chopped

50 g/*2 oz* pistachio nuts, chopped

a little plain flour

100 g/*4 oz* milk chocolate, melted

100 g/*4 oz* plain chocolate, grated

---

1 Whisk the egg white until stiff. Beat in the sugar. Fry the almonds quickly in the butter, add egg whites and sugar. Simmer, stirring for 5 minutes.

2 Add the cocoa, cinnamon, essence, brandy, lemon rinds and nuts. Fold in flour to bind.

3 Pipe 12 10 cm/4 inch sticks on to a greased baking sheet. Bake in a preheated oven at 180°C/350°F/gas mark 4 for 15 minutes.

4 When cold, dip into melted chocolate. Cover half with grated chocolate. *(centre)*

19

Christmas Triangles

Makes 36
Preparation time: 45 mins plus standing
180 kcal/755 kJ

For the dough:

400 g/14 oz honey

400 g/14 oz/3¹/₂ cups plain flour, sifted

*2.5 ml/¹/₂ **tsp** baking powder*

*30 ml/2 **tbsp** ground cinnamon*

*2.5 ml/¹/₂ **tsp** ground cardamom*

*2.5 ml/¹/₂ **tsp** ground coriander*

*2.5 ml/¹/₂ **tsp** grated nutmeg*

*10 ml/2 **tsp** grated lemon rind*

400 g/14 oz/3¹/₂ cups toasted almonds, coarsely chopped

For covering:

100 g/4 oz milk chocolate, melted

100 g/4 oz plain chocolate, melted

1 Boil up the honey then allow to cool. Work in the flour followed by the baking powder.
2 Knead in all the spices, the lemon rind and almonds.
3 Roll the dough out to 5 mm/¹/₄ in thick and transfer to a greased baking sheet. Bake in a preheated oven at 180°C/350°F/gas mark 4 for 15 minutes. Cut into 3.5 cm/1¹/₂ in wide strips then cut into about 36 triangles.

4 Coat with melted chocolate and leave on a wire rack to harden.

Photograph opposite (top)

Berlin Chocolate Bread

Makes 36
Preparation time: 1¹/₂ hours
350 kcal/1470 kJ

For the dough:

450 g/1 lb/4 cups plain flour

50 g/2 oz/¹/₂ cup cocoa powder

100 g/4 oz/1 cup walnuts, coarsely chopped

100 g/4 oz/1 cup hazel nuts, coarsely chopped

100 g/4 oz/1 cup peanuts, coarsely chopped

50 g/2 oz/1 cup pine kernels, coarsely chopped

50 g/2 oz/1 cup pistachio nuts, coarsely chopped

400 g/14 oz rusks, crumbled

100 g/4 oz/²/₃ cup chopped mixed peel

500 g/1 lb 2 oz/2¹/₄ cups caster sugar

150 g/5 oz/²/₃ cup butter or margarine

250 ml/8 fl oz/1 cup warm water

*5 ml/1 **tsp** bicarbonate of soda*

For covering:

100 g/4 oz bitter orange marmalade, heated and strained

*30 ml/2 **tbsp** orange liqueur*

350 g/12 oz milk chocolate cake covering, melted

1 Sift the flour with the cocoa powder into a bowl. Sprinkle with the nuts and crushed rusks. Add the mixed peel, sugar then the butter or margarine cut into small flakes.
2 Make a well in the centre and pour in the water, then sprinkle with bicarbonate of soda. Using a fork and working from the outside to the centre, mix to a pliable dough. Transfer to a bowl, cover with a cloth and refrigerate for at least 1 hour.
3 Divide into three equal parts and roll into sticks. Transfer to a baking sheet lined with greaseproof paper. Flatten each piece slightly then bake in a preheated oven at 220°C/425°F/gas mark 7 for 15 to 20 minutes. Cool on a wire rack.
4 Reheat the marmalade with the orange liqueur, spread over the cold loaves then cover with chocolate icing. Leave to dry completely and cut into 3 cm/1¹/₂ in wide strips.

Photograph opposite (bottom)

Half Moons

Makes 18 pairs
Preparation time: 40 mins
480 kcal/2010 kJ

For the dough:

100 g/**4 oz**/1 cup hazel nuts, ground

100 g/**4 oz**/1 cup ground almonds

100 g/**4 oz** marzipan

50 g/**2 oz**/¹/₄ cup cocoa powder

100 g/**4 oz** chopped mixed peel

30 ml/**2 tbsp** white rum

4 egg whites

400 g/**14 oz**/1³/₄ cups caster sugar

For the filling and covering:

45 ml/**3 tbsp** apricot jam

10 ml/**2 tsp** apricot liqueur

100 g/**4 oz** plain chocolate, melted

1 Knead the hazel nuts and almonds into the marzipan then work in the cocoa powder, the chopped peel and the rum. Add the egg whites and sugar and knead to a smooth dough.
2 Roll out on a floured surface to 5 mm/¹/₄ in thick and cut into half-moon shapes. Transfer to a baking tray lined with non-stick baking parchment in a preheated oven at 180°C/350°F/gas mark 4 for 10 to 15 minutes.
3 Mix the jam with the liqueur and use to sandwich together the biscuits. Coat with melted chocolate and leave to harden.

Photograph (bottom)

Meringue Tarts

Makes 12
Preparation time: 1 hour
plus drying
550 kcal/2310 kJ

---

5 egg whites

---

400 g/14 oz/1³/₄ cups caster sugar

---

100 g/4 oz plain chocolate, finely grated

---

250 ml/8 fl oz/1 cup double cream

---

200 g/7 oz milk chocolate, grated

---

5 ml/1 tsp vanilla essence

---

5 ml/1 tsp ground cinnamon

---

200 g/7 oz strawberries

---

225 g/8 oz redcurrant jelly, half melted

---

100 g/4 oz/1 cup toasted almonds, chopped

---

a few walnut halves

---

cocoa powder

---

1 Whisk the egg whites until stiff. Beat in two-thirds of the sugar until shiny and thick. Fold in the rest of the sugar with the grated chocolate. Pipe 24 ovals of meringue on lined baking trays. Dry out for about 3 hours in an oven at 120°C/250°F/gas mark ¹/₂.
2 Melt the cream and chocolate. Mix in the vanilla essence and cinnamon then cool. When cold whip, until thick.
3 Mix the jelly and sliced strawberries. Sandwich the ovals with strawberries and whipped chocolate. Decorate with remaining cream chocolate, almonds, walnut halves and cocoa powder.

Photograph (top)

Chocolate Double Deckers

Makes 18
Preparation time: 45 mins
145 kcal/610 kJ

150 g/5 oz/²⁄₃ cup butter
150 g/5 oz/³⁄₄ cup icing sugar
150 g/5 oz/1¹⁄₄ cups plain flour, sifted
5 ml/1 tsp vanilla essence
100 g/4 oz milk chocolate, grated
150 g/5 oz marzipan
50 g/2 oz/¹⁄₃ cup icing sugar, sifted
30 ml/2 tbsp Amaretto
1 egg white
200 g/7 oz milk chocolate, melted
50 g/2 oz/¹⁄₂ cup toasted flaked almonds

1 Beat the butter and icing sugar until creamy then work in the flour, essence and chocolate.
2 Pipe 36 round biscuits on to a lined baking tray. Bake in a preheated oven at 200°C/400°F/gas mark 6 for 10 minutes.
3 Knead the marzipan with the icing sugar and fold in the Amaretto and egg white. Sandwich the biscuits with the marzipan mixture.
4 Spread each sandwich thickly with melted chocolate and leave on a wire rack. Sprinkle with the almonds then leave until the chocolate hardens.

Photograph opposite (top)

Chocolate Pyramid

Serves 12
Preparation time: 1¹⁄₂ hours
640 kcal/2690 kJ

For the cake:
5 eggs, separated
2.5 ml/¹⁄₂ tsp lemon juice
100 g/4 oz/¹⁄₂ cup caster sugar
5 ml/1 tsp grated lemon rind
5 ml/1 tsp vanilla essence
75 g/3 oz/²⁄₃ cup plain flour
50 g/2 oz/¹⁄₂ cup cornflour
a pinch of baking powder
For the cream:
500 ml/17 fl oz/2¹⁄₄ cups milk
100 g/4 oz/¹⁄₂ cup caster sugar
25 g/1 oz/¹⁄₄ cup cocoa powder
50 g/2 oz/¹⁄₂ cup cornflour
2 eggs, beaten
10 ml/2 tsp ground cinnamon
15 ml/1 tbsp gelatine
45 ml/3 tbsp cold water
400 g/14 oz/1³⁄₄ cups butter
15 ml/1 tbsp coffee powder
For the covering:
225 g/8 oz marzipan
100 g/4 oz/²⁄₃ cup icing sugar, sifted
15 ml/1 tbsp cocoa powder
100 g/4 oz milk chocolate, melted

1 Whisk the egg whites with the lemon juice until stiff then beat in the sugar. Stir together the egg yolks, lemon rind and vanilla essence. Add to the whites.
2 Sieve the flour with the cornflour and baking powder, sprinkle over the egg mixture and carefully fold in with a metal spoon. Spread over a large lined Swiss roll tin. Bake in a preheated oven at 180°C/350°F/gas mark 4 for 20 minutes.
3 Bring half the milk to the boil with the sugar and cocoa. Blend the cornflour with the rest of the milk. Gradually add to the boiling milk, whisking until the mixture reboils. Simmer for 1 minute then beat in the eggs and cinnamon.
4 Soften the gelatine in cold water for 5 minutes, pour into a saucepan and melt over a very low heat. Cool. Beat the butter until fluffy and fold in the cocoa mixture a tablespoon at a time. Beat in the gelatine and coffee.
5 Cut the cake base into 5 wide strips, then cut 2 of the strips lengthways again. Arrange 6 strips in a pyramid, spreading the gelatine cream between the strips. Place the pyramid on the seventh biscuit strip and cover with the rest of the cream.
6 Knead the marzipan with the icing sugar and cocoa. Roll out thinly, cover the pyramid, then coat with chocolate.

Photograph opposite (bottom)

24

Chocolate Cream Log

Serves 12
Preparation time: 1¹/₂-2 hours
490 kcal/2060 kJ

For the cake:

4 eggs

100 g/4 oz/¹/₂ cup caster sugar

50 g/2 oz/¹/₂ cup flour

50 g/2 oz/¹/₂ cup cornflour

30 ml/2 tbsp cocoa powder

For the cream and decoration:

500 ml/17 fl oz/2¹/₄ cups milk

100 g/4 oz/¹/₂ cup caster sugar

50 g/2 oz/¹/₂ cup cornflour

5 ml/1 tsp vanilla essence

1 egg, beaten

400 g/14 oz/1³/₄ cups butter

100 g/4 oz plain chocolate, melted

chocolate flakes, crumbled

1 Put the eggs and sugar into a basin standing over a pan of simmering water. Beat until thick, rather like whipped cream. Sift the flour with the cornflour and cocoa powder. Gradually fold into the egg mixture using a metal spoon.

2 Transfer to a large Swiss roll tin lined with non-stick baking parchment. Quickly spread smooth with a palette knife then bake in a preheated oven at 200°C/400°F/gas mark 6 for 15 to 20 minutes. Cool on a rack. Remove the paper.

3 Bring half the milk to the boil with the sugar. Blend the cornflour smoothly with the rest of the milk, pour into the boiling milk and bring to the boil, stirring continuously. Stir in the vanilla essence and the egg. Remove from the heat and leave to cool completely.

4 Beat the butter until creamy and carefully fold in the cold cornflour mixture. Gradually stir in the melted chocolate.

5 Spread the chocolate cream over the cake before it has cooled completely then roll up. Cut a slice from both ends and arrange on top of the roll to look like branches. Cover completely with the rest of chocolate cream, 'comb' with a fork to give the log a bark-like appearance. Sprinkle the lower half of the side with chocolate flakes. Leave the log to cool completely in the refrigerator before slicing.

Truffle Gâteau

Serves 16
Preparation time: 2 hours
630 kcal/2640 kJ

For the cake:

75 g/**3 oz**/¹/₃ cup butter

8 egg yolks

5 egg whites

75 g/**3 oz**/¹/₃ cup caster sugar

75 g/**3 oz**/²/₃ cup plain flour

30 ml/**2 tbsp** cornflour

15 ml/**1 tbsp** cocoa powder

For the filling and decoration:

500 ml/**17 fl oz**/2¹/₄ cups double cream

600 g/**1¹/₂ lb** plain chocolate, grated

4.5 ml/**3 tbsp** rum

150 g/**5 oz** marzipan

175 g/**6 oz**/1 cup icing sugar

20 ml/**4 tsp** cocoa powder

200 g/**7 oz** milk chocolate, melted

roses made from marzipan or sugar

1 chocolate flake, crumbled

1 Beat the butter and the egg yolks until fluffy. Whisk the egg whites until very stiff, stir in the sugar, then fold into the egg yolk mixture. Sieve the flour with the cornflour and cocoa powder over the mixture. Stir lightly with a metal spoon until evenly blended.
2 Spread one-fifth of the mixture into a 25 cm/10 in greased sandwich tin lined with non-stick baking parchment. Bake in a preheated oven at 180°C/350°F/gas mark 4 for 10 minutes. Make 4 more cakes in the same way.
3 Bring the cream, chocolate and rum to the boil, stirring continuously. Cool completely then whisk until thick.
4 Sandwich the layers of cake together with the chocolate cream, spreading remainder over top and sides.
5 Knead the marzipan with the icing sugar and cocoa powder, roll out thinly and use to cover the gâteau. Coat with melted chocolate.
6 After cooling, decorate with roses and any remaining chocolate cream. Decorate the lower edge with the chocolate flakes.

Photograph opposite (top)

Chocolate Gâteau

Serves 16
Preparation time: 1¹/₂ hours
360 kcal/1510 kJ

For the cake:

150 g/**5 oz**/²/₃ cup butter

150 g/**5 oz**/²/₃ cup caster sugar

8 eggs, separated

150 g/**5 oz** plain chocolate, melted

30 ml/**2 tbsp** icing sugar, sieved

150 g/**5 oz**/1¹/₄ cups plain flour

5 ml/**1 tsp** baking powder

225 g/**8 oz** orange marmalade, warmed

45 ml/**3 tbsp** orange liqueur

200 g/**7 oz** plain chocolate cake covering, melted

marzipan leaves

1 chocolate flake, crumbled

1 Beat the butter and sugar until creamy. Fold in the egg yolks and the melted chocolate. Whisk the egg whites until stiff, fold in the icing sugar then combine with the egg yolk mixture, stirring lightly until smooth. Sieve the flour with the baking powder and, using a large metal spoon, fold into the egg mixture.
2 Spread into a 23 cm/9 in round tin, buttered and paper-lined. Bake in a preheated oven at 180°C/350°F/gas mark 4 for 25 to 30 minutes. Cool on a wire rack. Halve horizontally when completely cold.
3 Flavour the marmalade with the liqueur. Spread most of it over the bottom half of the cake then place the second half on top. Brush the top and sides with the rest of the marmalade.
4 Cover the gâteau with the melted chocolate icing. Leave the gâteau to dry completely, place the marzipan leaves on top and finally decorate the edge of the gâteau with the chocolate flakes.

Photograph opposite (bottom)

Confectionery

In this chapter you will find a selection of delightful and very special sweets and confections. Some will take a little time and care, but they make the perfect conclusion to a dinner party or wonderful gifts for your friends.

Dessert Biscuits

Makes 36
Preparation time: 2 hours
300 kcal/1260 kJ

For the dough:

300 g/**11** oz/2¾ cups plain flour

225 g/**8** oz/1 cup butter, slightly softened

100 g/**4** oz/¹⁄₂ cup caster sugar

1 egg, beaten

5 ml/**1 tsp** vanilla essence

10 ml/**2 tsp** finely grated lemon rind

a pinch of salt

For the filling and coating:

250 g/**9** oz truffles

225 g/**8** oz/1 cup butter, slightly softened

50 g/**2** oz/¹⁄₂ cup blanched almonds, split

50 g/**2** oz/¹⁄₂ cup hazel nuts, halved

200 g/**7** oz milk chocolate, melted

50 g/**2** oz plain chocolate, melted

1 Sift the flour into a bowl. Rub in the butter and sugar. Knead lightly to a pliable dough with the egg, vanilla essence, lemon rind and salt.
2 Wrap in foil and rest in the refrigerator for 1 to 1¹⁄₂ hours.
3 Roll out the dough on a floured work surface and cut into 36 assorted shapes. Arrange on a baking tray lined with non-stick baking parchment and bake in a preheated oven at 180°C/350°F/gas mark 4 for 10 to 15 minutes.
4 Soften the truffles and beat until creamy with the softened butter. Pipe on to the biscuits then dot each here and there with almonds and hazel nuts. Transfer to a wire rack and leave in a cool place until the truffle mixture hardens. Coat each with milk chocolate and leave to harden. Finally decorate with plain chocolate as shown in the picture.

Photograph opposite (left)

Almond Nibbles

Makes 36
Preparation time: 40 mins
90 kcal/380 kJ

225 g/**8** oz/2 cups large almonds

100 g/**4** oz/²⁄₃ cup icing sugar, sifted

200 g/**7** oz milk chocolate

50 g/**2** oz/¹⁄₂ cup cocoa powder, sifted

50 g/**2** oz/¹⁄₂ cup icing sugar, sifted

1 Spread the almonds over a baking tray, sprinkle with icing sugar and bake in a preheated oven at 200°C/400°F/gas mark 6 until the sugar has melted. Remove and leave to cool. Transfer to a bowl.
2 Melt the chocolate and pour over the almonds. Toss until the chocolate firms up. Coat half the almonds in cocoa powder and the remainder with icing sugar.

Photograph opposite (right)

Bubbly Truffles

Makes 36
Preparation time: 50 mins
180 kcal/755 kJ

---

500 ml/*18 fl oz*/*2¹/₄ cups*
sparkling white wine

---

100 g/*4 oz* honey

---

500 g/*1 lb 2 oz* plain
chocolate, grated

---

300 g/*10 oz* milk chocolate,
grated

---

100 g/*4 oz*/*¹/₂ cup butter*

For coating:

---

200 g/*7 oz* milk chocolate,
melted

---

100 g/*4 oz*/*¹/₂ cup caster*
sugar

---

1 Bring the wine and
honey to the boil. Add the
plain and milk chocolate,
with the butter and melt
over a low heat, stirring
continuously. Leave the
mixture to cool.
2 Transfer to a piping bag
and pipe cherry-sized
mounds on to a sheet of
greaseproof paper. Leave
to cool completely.
3 Cover in melted milk
chocolate, roll in caster
sugar and leave to dry
completely.

Photograph (bottom left)

34

Butter Truffles

Makes 36
Preparation time: 50 mins
140 kcal/590 kJ

120 ml/**4 fl oz**/¹/₂ *cup cream*
100 g/**4 oz**/¹/₂ *cup butter*
300 g/**10 oz** *milk chocolate, grated*
100 g/**4 oz** *chocolate truffles*
10 ml/**2 tsp** *vanilla essence*
a few drops of rum flavouring
For coating:
200 g/**7 oz** *white chocolate, melted*

1 Bring the cream and butter to the boil. Add the milk chocolate and truffles and melt over a low heat, stirring continuously. Stir in the vanilla essence and the rum flavouring.
2 Leave the mixture to cool a little then transfer to a piping bag. Pipe cherry-sized mounds on to greaseproof paper and leave to cool completely.
3 Roll the mounds into little balls, coat with the white chocolate and dry on a wire rack. Leave until the chocolate hardens before serving.

Photograph (top right)

Rum Truffles

Makes 36
Preparation time: 50 mins
165 kcal/695 kJ

---

500 g/1 lb 2 oz/plain chocolate, grated

250 ml/8 fl oz/1 cup whipping cream

50 g/2 oz/¹/₄ cup butter

250 ml/8 fl oz/1 cup rum

30 ml/2 tbsp brandy

10 ml/2 tsp ground cinnamon

10 ml/2 tsp grated orange rind

10 ml/2 tsp vanilla essence

36 Maraschino cherries

200 g/7 oz chocolate vermicelli

---

1 Put the chocolate, cream and butter into a saucepan and melt over a very low heat, stirring continuously. Mix in the rum, brandy, cinnamon, orange rind and vanilla essence. Leave to cool.
2 After the mixture is cool, transfer to a piping bag and pipe 36 mounds on to a sheet of greaseproof paper. Dry the Maraschino cherries with kitchen towel and place a cherry on each mound.
3 Roll the cherries and the chocolate mounds into little balls, coat with the chocolate vermicelli and leave to dry completely.

Photograph opposite (top)

Marzipan Bars

Makes 36
Preparation time: 40 mins
195 kcal/820 kJ

---

500 g/1 lb 2 oz marzipan

450 g/1 lb/2²/₃ cups icing sugar, sifted

For the nut bars:

50 g/2 oz plain chocolate

30 ml/2 tbsp chopped almonds

30 ml/2 tbsp chopped pistachio nuts

30 ml/2 tbsp chopped walnuts

30 ml/2 tbsp white rum

For the fruit bars:

60 ml/4 tbsp chopped mixed peel

1 knob of preserved ginger, chopped

1 slice candied pineapple, finely chopped

30 ml/2 tbsp orange liqueur

For the cracknel bars:

30 ml/2 tbsp brittle nut crunch, crushed

30 ml/2 tbsp chopped raisins

30 ml/2 tbsp brandy

For coating:

75 g/3 oz white chocolate, melted

75 g/3 oz milk chocolate, melted

75 g/3 oz plain chocolate, melted

---

1 Knead the marzipan smoothly with the icing sugar and divide into three equal portions.
2 Knead one-third of the marzipan with the melted chocolate, almonds, pistachio nuts, walnuts and rum. When evenly combined and holding together, cut into 12 bars.
3 Knead the next third of the marzipan with the mixed peel, ginger, pineapple and orange liqueur. When evenly combined and holding together, cut into 12 bars.
4 Knead the last third of the marzipan with the nut crunch, raisins and brandy. When evenly combined and holding together, cut into 12 bars.
5 Coat 12 bars with white chocolate, 12 bars with milk chocolate and 12 bars with plain chocolate. Leave to harden on a wire rack.

Photograph opposite (bottom)

Desserts

Lovers of chocolate can delight in these marvellously tempting recipes to complete a perfect meal.

Chocolate Mousse

Serves 4
Preparation time: 30 mins
plus standing
855 kcal/3580 kJ

5 eggs, separated

100 g/4 oz/²/₃ cup icing sugar, sifted

30 ml/2 tbsp brandy

60 ml/4 tbsp strong black coffee

100 g/4 oz/¹/₂ cup butter, melted

175 g/6 oz plain chocolate, melted

For decoration:

150 ml/¹/₄ pt/²/₃ cup double cream

5 ml/1 tsp vanilla essence

1 chocolate flake, crumbled

1 Mix the egg yolks with the icing sugar, brandy and coffee in a basin standing over a saucepan of simmering water. Beat until thick. Melt the butter and chocolate in 2 separate bowls.
2 Add the melted butter and chocolate to the egg yolk mixture, stirring until smooth. Leave to cool.
3 Whisk the egg whites until very stiff and fold into the cold chocolate mixture. Transfer to 4 glasses and chill overnight.
4 Whisk the cream with the vanilla essence until stiff. Use to decorate each mousse then sprinkle with chocolate flakes.

Photograph opposite (top)

Chocolate Pears

Serves 4
Preparation time: 25 mins
plus standing
650 kcal/2730 kJ

4 large pears

250 ml/8 fl oz/1 cup white wine

juice of 1 lemon

1 stick cinnamon

a few cloves

5 ml/1 tsp vanilla essence

a little sugar

250 ml/8 fl oz/1 cup pear liqueur or kirsch

200 g/7 oz plain chocolate, melted

vanilla ice cream (see following recipe)

250 ml/8 fl oz/1 cup double cream, stiffly whipped

grated plain chocolate

1 Carefully peel the pears, leaving the stalks on the fruit. Using a corer, remove the core from below. Put the wine into a saucepan with the lemon juice, cinnamon, cloves and essence. Sweeten with sugar to taste.
2 Add the pears, cover and simmer for 10 minutes. Drain well, then sprinkle with liqueur. Cover and leave overnight in a cool place.
3 Next day, dip the pears in the melted chocolate, leave to dry and arrange on the ice cream. Decorate with whipped cream and grated chocolate.

Photograph opposite (centre)

Vanilla Ice Cream

Serves 4

2 eggs

1 egg yolk

175 g/6 oz/1 cup icing sugar, sifted

5 ml/1 tsp vanilla essence

250 ml/4 fl oz/1 cup whipping cream

1 Beat the eggs with the egg yolk, icing sugar and vanilla essence until fluffy. Whip the cream until stiff and mix carefully with the whisked egg mixture. Put into a freezing mould and freeze for 2 to 3 hours, stirring a few times before the ice cream hardens. Keep the mould covered to avoid ice crystals forming on top.
2 The ice cream can be enhanced by adding grated hazel nuts, liqueur or grated chocolate.

White Chocolate Parfait

Serves 4
Preparation time: 1 hour
plus freezing
430 kcal/1110 kJ

---

4 egg yolks

---

3 eggs

---

*175 g/**6 oz**/³/₄ cup caster sugar*

---

*60 ml/**4 tbsp** white rum*

---

*250 g/**9 oz** white chocolate, melted*

---

*250 ml/**8 fl oz**/1 cup double cream*

---

*10 ml/**2 tsp** vanilla essence*

---

24 Maraschino cherries

---

*100 g/**4 oz**/1 cup pistachio nuts, chopped*

1 Put the egg yolks, eggs, sugar and rum into a basin over a pan of simmering water. Whisk to a creamy consistency then fold in the melted chocolate. Remove from the heat and stir until cold.
2 Beat the cream with the vanilla essence until thick then fold carefully into the egg cream. Drain the Maraschino cherries thoroughly, chop and add to the cream mixture with the pistachio nuts.
3 Pack into a block mould, cover and freeze for 2 to 3 hours. Serve cut into slices.

Photograph (left)

Luxury Chocolate Ice Cream

Serves 12
Preparation time: 50 mins
plus freezing
280 kcal/1180 kJ

---

3 egg yolks

---

1 egg

---

*100 g/**4 oz**/¹/₂ cup caster sugar*

---

*250 ml/**8 fl oz**/1 cup milk*

---

*200 g/**7 oz** milk chocolate, grated*

---

*250 ml/**8 fl oz**/1 cup whipping cream*

---

*5 ml/**1 tsp** vanilla essence*

---

1 Bring the egg yolks, egg, sugar, milk and milk chocolate to the boil over a low heat, stirring all the time. Remove from the heat and cool completely.
2 Beat the cream with the vanilla essence until stiff then combine with the chocolate mixture. Transfer to a plastic container and freeze for 2 to 3 hours, stirring 2 or 3 times before the ice cream hardens. Keep covered in between to prevent ice crystals forming on the surface.

Photograph (right)

Chocolate Fruit Fondue

Serves 4
Preparation time: 15 mins
1110 kcal/4660 kJ

200 ml/7 fl oz/scant 1 cup double cream, whipped
200 g/7 oz milk chocolate, grated
200 g/7 oz plain chocolate, grated
5 ml/1 tsp vanilla essence
45 ml/3 tbsp white rum
5 ml/1 tsp grated lemon rind
For dipping:
1 banana, sliced
200 g/7 oz pineapple pieces
200 g/7 oz strawberries
200 g/7 oz lychees
100 g/4 oz little ratafia biscuits
500 g/1 lb 2 oz vanilla ice cream
100 g/4 oz raspberries, puréed
juice of 1 lemon

1 Heat the cream. Add the chocolate and continue to heat slowly until melted. Stir in the vanilla essence, rum and lemon rind.
2 Arrange the fruit and ratafias on plates. Scoop the vanilla ice cream into a bowl. Mix the raspberry purée with the lemon juice and pour over the ice cream.
3 Dip the fruit in the chocolate sauce and serve with the ice cream.

Photograph opposite (top)

Chocolate Shake

Serves 4
Preparation time: 15 mins
205 kcal/860 kJ

500 g/1 lb 2 oz chocolate ice cream
40 ml/4 tsp cocoa powder
5 ml/1 tsp ground cinnamon
60 ml/4 tbsp white rum
500 ml/17 fl oz/2¼ cups milk
For decoration:
a few strawberries
a few sprigs lemon balm

1 Put the chocolate ice cream into a blender with the cocoa powder, cinnamon, rum and milk. Purée until smooth then pour into 4 glasses.
2 Clean the strawberries, wash, drain well and attach to the rims of the glasses. Garnish drinks with lemon balm.

Photograph opposite (bottom left)

Coconut Drink

Serves 4
Preparation time: 15 mins
530 kcal/2225 kJ

500 g/1 lb 2 oz chocolate ice cream
4 glasses apricot juice (about teacup size)
60 ml/4 tbsp coconut liqueur
250 ml/8 fl oz/1 cup orange liqueur
300 ml/½ pt/1¼ cups whipping cream
For decoration:
some cherry brandy
100 g/4 oz/½ cup caster sugar
a few pineapple pieces
a few cherries
a few peach pieces
a few sprigs of mint

1 Put the chocolate ice cream into a blender with the apricot juice, coconut liqueur, orange liqueur and cream. Purée until smooth.
2 Dip the rims of 4 cocktail glasses in cherry brandy then in sugar. This will create a red crusty rim. Fill the glasses with the chocolate drink.
3 Skewer the pineapple, cherries and peach pieces onto 4 cocktail sticks. Place the sticks in the drinks, decorate with mint and serve immediately.

Photograph opposite (bottom right)

Chocolate Pudding

Serves 4
Preparation time: 1 hour
800 kcal/3350 kJ

For the pudding:

250 ml/8 fl oz/1 cup milk

75 g/3 oz/¹/₃ cup caster sugar

100 g/4 oz plain chocolate, broken into pieces

150 ml/¹/₄ pt/²/₃ cup double cream, whipped

5 ml/1 tsp grated lemon rind

1 packet custard powder

5 ml/1 tsp vanilla essence

30 ml/2 tbsp cocoa powder, sifted

60 ml/4 tbsp chocolate liqueur

For decoration:

1 pear, peeled

1 apple, peeled

100 g/4 oz strawberries

100 g/4 oz mixture of red and white grapes

150 ml/¹/₄ pt/²/₃ cup whipping cream

5 ml/1 tsp vanilla essence

30 ml/2 tbsp chocolate vermicelli

---

1 Pour the milk into a saucepan. Add the butter, sugar and chocolate and stir over a low heat until the chocolate melts. Add the cream and lemon rind. Mix the custard powder, vanilla essence, cocoa powder and chocolate liqueur smoothly together, adding 15–30 ml/1–2 tbsp of water, if the mixture seems too thick. Gradually add to the boiling milk mixture in the pan. Return to the boil, stirring continuously. Pour into a glass bowl, cover and cool.

2 Core the pear and the apple and cut into thin slices. Halve the strawberries and the grapes, removing the seeds. Arrange the fruit on the pudding.

3 Beat the cream with the vanilla essence until stiff then pipe decoratively on top of the pudding. Sprinkle with chocolate vermicelli.

Index of Recipes

foulsham
Yeovil Road, Slough, Berkshire, SL1 4JH

ISBN 0-572-01823-1

This English language edition copyright
© 1993 W. Foulsham & Co. Ltd
Originally published by Falken-Verlag
GmbH, Niedernhausen TS, Germany
Photographs copyright © Falken Verlag

Printed in Portugal